# Plague Plot

### Peter Brimacombe

THROUGHOUT HISTORY, Britain has been subject to outbreaks of serious fire and deadly disease. There have also been numerous plots attempting to topple the nation's rulers. Many of these dramatic incidents, some taking place many centuries ago, are still remembered today – cataclysmic disasters such as the Black Death and the Great Fire of London. The failure of the 1605 Gunpowder Plot is celebrated annually, while the abortive Jacobite uprising of 1745 assured the charismatic Charles Edward Stuart a permanent place in romantic folklore as Bonnie Prince Charlie.

These legendary occurrences certainly capture the imagination, but equally fascinating and significant are the causes and the long-term effect on the lives of ordinary people caught up in the consequences of extraordinary events.

Even in today's sophisticated world, fire can devastate historic buildings like York Minster and Windsor Castle. New diseases such as Aids demonstrate that, in spite of the advances in modern medicine, plague is by no means a thing of the past. The ruthless plots of terrorist groups continue to endanger the nation. Fire, plague and plot are as prevalent today as ever – terror in triplicate that is far from being confined to the history books.

Destruction by Fire of Both Houses of Parliament, *by H. O'Neill. The replacement buildings, by Sir Charles Barry, were in turn set on fire by German incendiary bombs during the Second World War.*

# A Legacy of Terror

ON SEVERAL OCCASIONS, fire has devastated large areas of central London, while periodically great buildings such as Hampton Court Palace, Windsor Castle, the Houses of Parliament, Uppark, Castle Howard and York Minster have been set ablaze and severely damaged. Fire was so common in the Tudor era that a specific type of confidence trickster, known as 'demanders of glimmer', preyed on unsuspecting victims by pretending that they had lost everything through fire. Fire brigades were non-existent until the end of the 17th century, and even today fire can quickly bring terror and destruction on a massive scale.

The plague, tuberculosis and smallpox have all been killer diseases in the past, proving fatal for notable characters such as Henry VII, Hans Holbein and Emily Brontë. The innocent sounding children's rhyme

'Ring a ring of roses,
A pocketful of posies,
Atishoo! Atishoo!
We all fall down'

was actually grimly symbolic of the plague. The 'ring of roses' referred to the telltale marks on a victim's body, posies of medicinal herbs were carried to ward off the plague, sneezing was a symptom of the disease, while falling down indicated the approach of death.

*In Albrecht Dürer's famous woodcut, The Four Horsemen of the Apocalypse (c.1504), the evils of death, war, famine and pestilence strike terror into men's hearts.*

BELOW: *Wat Tyler, leader of the late 14th-century Peasants' Revolt, is backed down and murdered by one of Richard II's knights during a parley between the young king and the rebel army at Smithfield, London.*

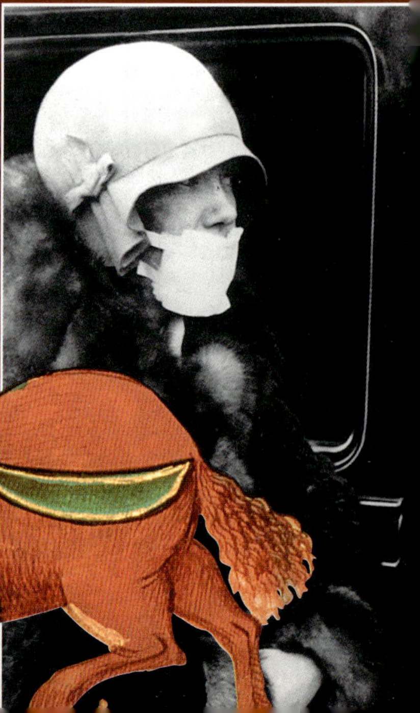

The list of plotters dedicated to bringing down the nation's leaders seems endless. Wat Tyler, William Wallace, Robert the Bruce, Perkin Warbeck, Owen Glendower, Guy Fawkes, the Duke of Monmouth, Bonnie Prince Charlie, William Joyce, and Burgess and Maclean are just some whose fanatical ideology has threatened the status quo – and sometimes succeeded. The Conservative Prime Minister Spencer Perceval was assassinated at the House of Commons in 1812. The IRA bombing of the Grand Hotel in Brighton in 1984 was the first attempt to blow up a government since Guy Fawkes – on this occasion the Conservative Prime Minister, Margaret Thatcher, narrowly escaped death. In former times it was usually only the nation's leaders who were targeted, but today's terrorists are often totally indiscriminate, so that the lives of ordinary people are threatened by extremism as never before – as instanced by the horrendous explosion on the Pan Am flight over Lockerbie in Scotland in 1988, when all 270 passengers on board lost their lives. Fire, plague and plot continue to menace society as much as in the past, equally terrifying, destructive and highly dangerous.

RIGHT: *Firefighters and rescue workers on a balcony outside Brighton's Grand Hotel following the IRA bomb attack on the 1984 Conservative Party Conference. A growing number of such attacks have terrorized the nation in recent years.*

BELOW: *The flu pandemic that broke out in 1918 killed more than 20 million people – incredibly, a greater number than perished during the First World War. Masks were worn as protection against the further outbreaks that continued into the early 1930s.*

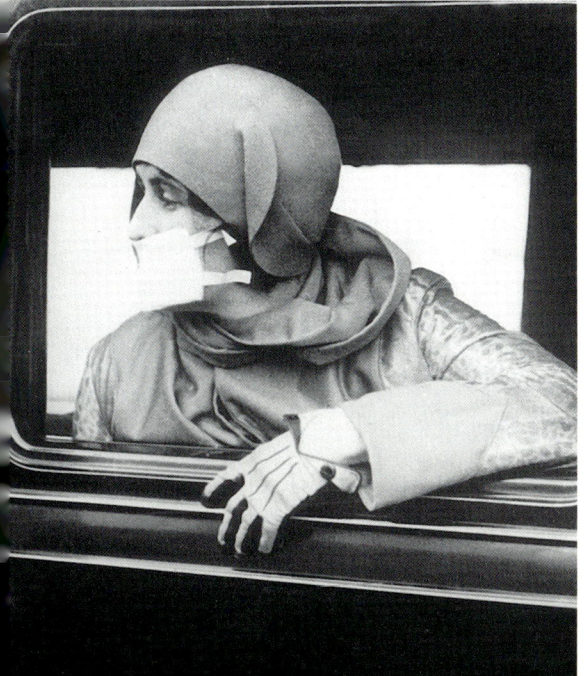

# The Great Fire of London

THE GREAT FIRE OF LONDON began during the early hours of Sunday morning, 2 September 1666, at a bakery in Pudding Lane in the heart of the City, the baker having failed to extinguish his oven properly before going to bed. The courtyard of the Star Inn next door was full of straw, and tons of highly inflammable goods lay in warehouses in nearby Thames Street. Flames spread rapidly through closely packed timber houses, fanned by a strong breeze. With no hoses or firemen, the resulting inferno quickly raged out of control. Wild rumours soon began to circulate that Catholics or foreigners were responsible.

Panic-stricken citizens fled through the narrow streets to escape the searing inferno, or scrambled aboard boats on the River Thames, carrying as many of their belongings as they could as fire engulfed their homes. Everywhere was scorching heat, roaring flames and smouldering ruins – 'the saddest sight of desolation that I ever saw,' declared Samuel Pepys, ever eager to record these dramatic events in his diary.

King Charles I remained in London, together with his brother the Duke of York. Regardless of their personal safety, they directed operations to demolish buildings in order to create firebreaks to check the fire's relentless progress. The Great Fire burned for four days and nights, only ceasing when the wind changed direction and the flames blew back over already devastated ground. By then the City, including St Paul's Cathedral, the Royal Exchange and the Guildhall, was a smouldering ruin. More than 13,000 houses had been destroyed and 100,000 people made homeless. Miraculously, no one was killed and a new City of London was soon to rise from the ashes; but its medieval heart was gone for ever.

*A view of St Paul's and the River Thames by an unknown Dutch artist depicting the horrific scene at the height of the fire, when all London seemed ablaze. 'One entire arch of fire … it made me weep to see it. The churches, houses and all on fire and flaming at once; and a horrid noise the flames made …' observed Pepys.*

## A MISSED OPPORTUNITY

Within a week of the fire dying out, Sir Christopher Wren presented the king with a visionary plan for a new City of London, with sweeping vistas, wide boulevards and elegant squares – a grand design that anticipated modern-day Paris or Washington. Sadly, however, the city merchants favoured a rapid return to the status quo in order to revive their financial fortunes. King Charles was not in a strong enough position to override them, so art gave way to commerce. Wren's vision was not fulfilled, apart from his sublime St Paul's Cathedral and the creation of a number of exquisite new churches.

King Charles responded heroically to the Great Fire, but left London during the plague to stay at Malmesbury House in Salisbury. However, he constantly rode around the town reassuring anxious citizens and calming their fears.

An early fire engine, built by John Keeling of London in 1678 in the wake of the Great Fire. To qualify for assistance, a citizen needed fire insurance and to display the sign of the phoenix on his building.

Johann B. Homann's view across the Thames from the South Bank, c.1730, shows Wren's St Paul's Cathedral and the steeples of numerous smaller churches – all that survived of Wren's ambitious vision of a new London.

# The Fires of War

IN 1941 THE GERMAN AIR FORCE carried out several heavy incendiary raids on the major naval port of Plymouth, attacking British warships moored in Devonport Dockyard to refuel, rearm and revictual. On 2 May Winston Churchill visited the port, going first to the docks, accompanied by the formidable Lady Astor, the first-ever woman Member of Parliament to enter the House of Commons, who was Plymouth's Lady Mayoress at that time. One of the naval blocks had suffered a direct hit and in the gymnasium there was the disturbing sight of a large number of coffins, separated only by a low curtain from 40 men lying badly injured. In the midst of such devastation there was really no alternative. The resources of the emergency services were stretched almost to breaking point and the outlook was indeed grim.

TOP RIGHT: *A lone milkman stoically continues his rounds among the rubble, graphically conveying the scale of Plymouth's devastation. Other regional ports such as Bristol, Liverpool, Portsmouth and Southampton also suffered severely.*

RIGHT: *Anxious citizens study the air-raid casualty lists at the height of the German Airforce attacks in 1941. It was but a short flight across the English Channel from airfields in Brittany, and civilian casualties mounted rapidly.*

ABOVE: *Churchill, complete with his characteristic cigar, inspects coastal defences in 1940, when invasion loomed following the fall of France and Britain stood alone against the might of the German war machine.*

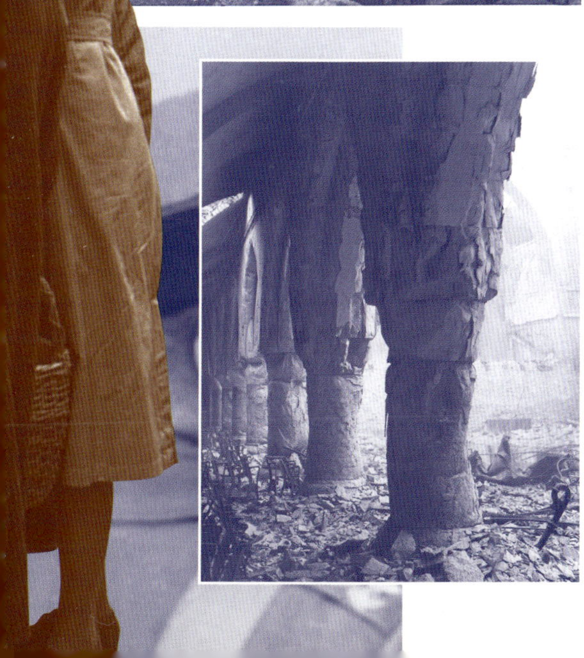

In the afternoon Churchill toured the city centre, which had suffered five heavy raids in just over a week. Hardly a house appeared to be habitable; everywhere lay huge piles of charred rubble, and the still-smouldering fires produced a huge cloud of menacing black smoke that hung over the city, darkening the sun and creating a pungent, acrid smell. The death toll was mounting, and the overall casualty rate grew remorselessly. Plymouth, like London and many other British cities at that time, appeared in grave danger of being reduced to a large heap of lifeless ashes. Much of Europe had been conquered by Hitler's seemingly invincible army; his panzers lay just across the English Channel, and the nation was under constant aerial bombardment.

The Prime Minister was very depressed – there were no stirring speeches or ringing Churchillian phrases. 'I have never seen the like,' he kept repeating plaintively to his long-serving Private Secretary, John Colville. Churchill appeared close to tears, but the feisty American-born Lady Astor chided him: 'Come along, Winston, this is no time for blubbing, things have got to be done.' Churchill never forgave her.

*The Cross of Nails, a symbol of reconciliation.*

### A CATHEDRAL RESTORED

The German air raid on Coventry in November 1940 severely damaged the city's medieval cathedral. Sir Basil Spence's post-war reconstruction ingeniously blended together the ruins, with surviving traditional features such as the late 14th-century steeple and strikingly modern design including the baptistry window by James Piper, Graham Sutherland's tapestry 'Christ in Glory' and Jacob Epstein's sculpture of *St Michael and the Devil* beside the vast entrance porch.

LEFT: *The ruins of the Guildhall in Plymouth as a result of a German air raid. Very few major centres of population in Britain escaped the avalanche of destruction that rained down from the skies.*

# Royal Palace Fires

Towards the end of the 17th century, flames engulfed the old Tudor palace at Whitehall, at one time the largest in Europe, destroying everything apart from the wine cellar and Inigo Jones's Banqueting Hall, added in 1619–22. Among the art treasures lost was Holbein's masterly mural of Henry VIII. Both William III and his wife, Queen Mary, disliked the palace intensely, so it was never rebuilt.

More recently, a terrible fire engulfed Sir Christopher Wren's King's Apartments at Hampton Court Palace, killing the occupant of the 'grace-and-favour' apartment above, where the fire started. Following a six-year restoration, the King's Apartments were reopened by Her Majesty Queen Elizabeth II on 8 July 1992, just a few months before an even more dramatic royal palace fire would occur.

During the winter of 1992, the Upper Ward of Windsor Castle, a royal residence for more than 800 years, was undergoing extensive rewiring and refurbishment. On the morning of 20 November, picture restorers working in the private chapel noticed flames flickering above the curtains in front of the altar. The fire spread

TOP: *A new stained-glass window in St George's Chapel at Windsor Castle, installed in 1997. In the Private Chapel, where the fire had begun, the new altar was designed by Her Majesty Queen Elizabeth II's nephew, David Linley.*

ABOVE: *The charred interior of the Cartoon Gallery at Hampton Court Palace in 1986 illustrates the awesome damage that a fire can inflict. A hundred years earlier, 40 rooms north of Chapel Court had been seriously damaged by fire.*

rapidly through the roof voids, engulfing St George's Hall, the State and Octagon Dining Rooms, the Grand Reception Room and the Crimson Drawing Room, as well as more than 100 other rooms. By nightfall, temperatures had reached 1,500 degrees Fahrenheit (815 degrees Celsius). The Brunswick Tower and the Prince of Wales Tower were giant flaming torches, and melted lead ran like molten wax.

Prince Charles arrived in the evening. 'I went up to the roof above the Clock Tower – a terrible view … it was shattering, awful,' said the heir to the throne.

Miraculously, remarkably few valuable works of art or other treasures were lost, owing to the heroic efforts of castle staff, soldiers, and anyone else in the vicinity. Priceless Canalettos, Van Dycks, Leonardo drawings, Gobelin tapestries, Sèvres porcelain and Pugin chairs were carried to safety.

More than 200 firefighters with 36 fire engines used nearly one and a half million gallons of water to contain the blaze. By the time it was extinguished 15 hours later, more than £36 million worth of damage had been done. No wonder The Queen referred to 1992 as her *annus horribilis* in her annual speech at the Guildhall.

## RESTORATION

Plans for the restoration of Windsor Castle ranged from maintaining an evocative ruin to creating a strikingly modern design. A traditional solution was preferred, largely replacing the original, apart from Giles Downes' neo-Gothic St George's Hall, which represents a radical improvement on Wyatville's unsatisfactory box-like interior. Restoration represented a major challenge to the numerous craftsmen and contractors involved, but by the fifth anniversary of the fire, and the 50th anniversary of the wedding of Her Majesty The Queen and the Duke of Edinburgh, the work was complete.

*Firemen tackle the huge fire at Windsor Castle in 1992. Although the fire caused millions of pounds worth of damage, no lives were lost and fire was prevented from spreading further by the fire brigades' prompt and skilful efforts.*

LEFT: *A coloured engraving c.1700 of the Palace at Whitehall before it was almost completely destroyed by fire in 1698, from* A Book of the Prospects of the Remarkable Places in and about the City of London.

# The Black Death

THE BLACK DEATH – 'the pestilence that walketh in darkness' – devastated England for some 30 years in the mid 14th century, killing off more than one third of the population. It had arrived from the East, via the great trading routes, and was essentially a virulent pneumonic disease, highly contagious, causing acute inflammation of the lungs and invariably resulting in an agonizing death as the luckless victims coughed uncontrollably before drowning in their own phlegm.

The entire population was petrified by its sudden arrival, by its mysterious nature, and by the sheer helplessness of not knowing how to deal with it, there being no known cure. No one knew 'whence it cometh, whereof it arriveth and wherefore it is sent', but in the highly charged moral atmosphere of medieval England it was popularly believed that the Black Death had been sent by God as a punishment for human wickedness. Sin was indeed mortal, and whole communities perished. The shadow of the Grim Reaper stalked the land, clad in black cloak and brandishing his sharp scythe – a sinister symbol of death harvesting human souls.

ABOVE: An enlarged view of the rat flea Zenopsylla Choepis, responsible for spreading the bacteria that caused the bubonic plague prevalent, with pneumonic plague, during the Black Death.

ABOVE: Victims of the plague were buried in mass graves. The death toll was horrendous – there were lawsuits where all involved died before the cases could be heard, and almost everyone lost a relative or friend.

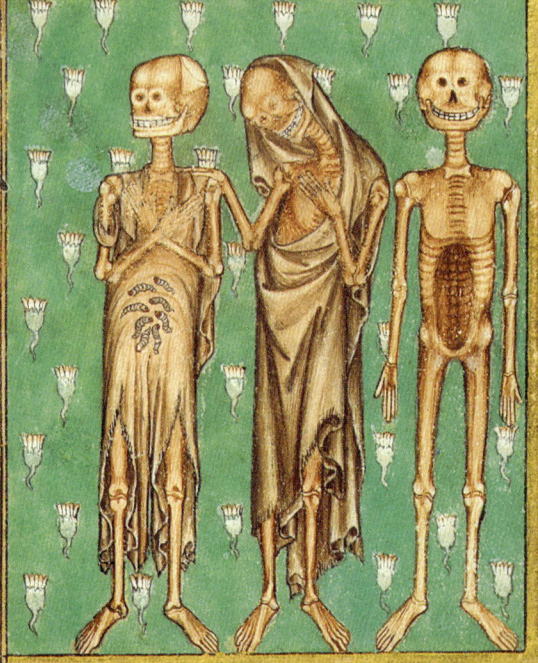

ABOVE: A macabre work entitled The Three Living and Three Dead. There were many gruesome sights during the Black Death, such as processions of flagellants, each whipping the person in front while chanting a dismal dirge.

## THE AFTERMATH

More than two centuries passed before the population regained its pre-Black Death level. A whole generation of skilled craftsmen had been wiped out, greatly affecting the development of Gothic architecture. Numbers in monastic communities never recovered. The nation's economy stood still. The social upheaval that resulted culminated in the Peasants' Revolt, led by Wat Tyler and Jack Straw, in 1381. Today, more than six centuries later, the Black Death, so called because of the manner in which a corpse turned black with rapid putrefaction, is still regarded with a mixture of awe, horror and revulsion.

ABOVE: *A priest blesses plague-infected monks, from an illuminated mid 14th-century work in the British Library in London. In some monasteries, more than half the community perished as a result of the Black Death.*

The Black Death was a catastrophe of biblical proportions, affecting the entire nation. Whole towns and villages were abandoned, the houses empty save for rotting corpses covered in flies that gorged themselves on the putrid flesh. The countryside was devoid of human activity, fields were silent and deserted, cattle untended, crops withering away. Everywhere there was the stench of death and a climate of fear, misery and despair.

ABOVE: *Chaucer, the greatest literary figure of the age. In a twist of fate, Chaucer's sister-in-law married John of Gaunt, whose first wife died of the plague. The Tudor line came from this union – so without the Black Death, there might have been no Tudor monarchs.*

# The Great Plague

ON A SWELTERING SUMMER'S DAY in 1665, Samuel Pepys was horrified to see houses in Drury Lane with large red crosses painted on their doors. Bubonic plague had returned to London, a dreaded disease transmitted by fleas carried on the black rats that thrived in the appallingly filthy city. Dark red blotches all over the body led to high fever, delirium and agonizing death. There was no known cure, and the Lord Mayor unwittingly compounded the problem when, mistakenly believing that cats and dogs would spread the plague, he ordered their destruction, thereby eliminating the rats' main predators.

The death toll mounted rapidly. By August it had risen to 1,000 a day, and hundreds of bodies were heaped in huge pits. Crowds of spectators, including women and children, gathered at the scene of these mass burials to stare down with morbid fascination at the twisted piles of corpses below. Many people fled the city, including King Charles. Daniel Defoe's *Journal of the Plague Year* graphically describes a deserted city where all normal life had ceased and dense black smoke billowed from huge bonfires lit in an attempt to purify the air. Corpses littered the empty streets, which were uncannily silent. By the time the winter cold ended this calamity, it was estimated that more than 100,000 people had died.

LEFT: *This plague doctor, clad in protective mask and gown – which makes him look like a giant vulture hovering over a hapless victim – is from the London Dungeon's Great Plague exhibition. Definitely not for the faint-hearted!*

ABOVE: *The Plague Window at St Lawrence Church in Eyam features George Viccars, the first victim, surrounded by grieving neighbours. The church also has an illuminated list of the many villagers that succumbed to the plague.*

The Great Plague was not confined to London. On 7 September it claimed its first victim in the remote Derbyshire village of Eyam, carried there, it is believed, by fleas in a batch of cloth sent from London to the local tailor. Soon several neighbours died, and it was realized that Eyam was in the grip of a major epidemic.

William Mompesson, the young, newly appointed parson, persuaded the villagers to isolate themselves from the outside world in order to safeguard the rest of Derbyshire. This heroic act showed considerable courage and Christian generosity. By the time the plague ended 14 months later, more than 250 villagers – over one third of the population – had perished, including the parson's wife, Catherine. Her grave lies in the village churchyard. A special service is held in Eyam every year, on the last Sunday in August, to commemorate this remarkable act of self-sacrifice.

ABOVE: *This 17th-century woodcut, entitled* Bring Out Your Dead, *depicts the grisly sight of corpses being collected for burial – 'little noise heard day or night but the tolling of bells,' declared Pepys.*

### PLAGUE REMEDY

'If there doe a Botch appeare: Take a Pigeon and plucke the feathers off her Taile, very bare, and set her Taile to the sore, and thee will draw out the venom till she die; then take another and set too likewise, continuing so till the venome be drawne out, which you will see by the Pigeons, for they will die with the venome as long as there is any in (the Tumour); also a chicken or henne is very good.'

ABOVE: *The Great Plague of 1665 was not the only one in 17th-century London. There had been a severe outbreak in 1603, and this pamphlet – 'Gods Tokens of his feareful Judgements' – refers to one in 1625.*

ABOVE LEFT: *This illustration, from the ballad 'The famous ratketcher with his travels into France and his return to London', shows a rat-catcher in Tudor times, when the Royal Rat-catcher was a vital member of the Court.*

# A Royal Victim

IN THE 16TH CENTURY, smallpox was as much feared as the plague, being highly contagious and invariably proving fatal, particularly among women; so when in October 1562 Queen Elizabeth I succumbed to this terrible disease, the whole of the Royal Court was plunged into a profound sense of gloom and despondency. 'Last night the people were all in mourning for her as if she were already dead,' the Spanish ambassador reported gleefully to King Philip II, his sovereign in Madrid.

Elizabeth lay in a coma at Hampton Court Palace, surrounded by anxious members of her Privy Council. Pragmatic as ever, they quietly discussed potential successors to the throne in the event of the queen failing to recover. Elizabeth suddenly regained consciousness and, peering up at the blurred circle of concerned faces, deliriously muttered that she would like them to appoint her long-time favourite, Sir Robert Dudley, as Lord Protector of the Realm, hastily adding that although she had always loved Dudley dearly, there had never been any impropriety in their relationship. She then lost consciousness again, leaving her Privy Council in a state of severe shock.

In a desperate attempt to find a cure, the council sent for Dr Burcot, a German physician and reputed expert in dealing with smallpox. Burcot wrapped the still-unconscious queen in a scarlet blanket and gently laid her down on the floor in front of the huge fire burning brightly in her room, which gave out colossal heat. Amazingly, this bizarre remedy proved highly successful and Elizabeth made a complete recovery, much to the nation's delight. A moment of huge crisis for both the queen and country had passed, and Elizabethan England went on to greatness and glory – thanks to Dr Burcot, an unsung hero of English history.

LEFT: *Queen Elizabeth I, painted around the time that she caught smallpox. The wife of the Duke of Bedford, a member of her Privy Council, had recently died of the disease, so the Royal Court was in despair.*

ABOVE: *This illustration of a physician – not looking particularly well himself – is from Bullein's* Bulwarke of Defense against All Sickness, *published in 1562, the year Queen Elizabeth I contracted smallpox.*

ABOVE: *Apothecary's jars from the 16th century, from the Shakespeare Birthplace Trust at Stratford-upon-Avon. Shakespeare's son-in-law, John Hall, was a doctor and today Hall's Croft, his former home, has a dispensary displayed as in Shakespeare's time.*

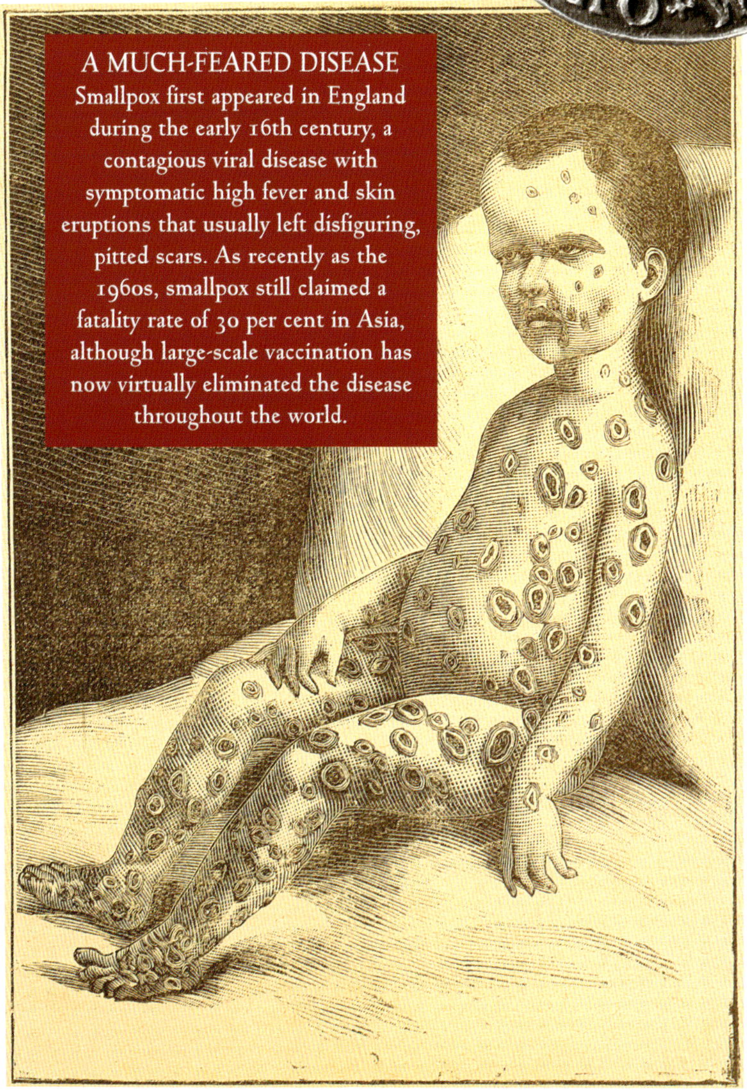

## A MUCH-FEARED DISEASE

Smallpox first appeared in England during the early 16th century, a contagious viral disease with symptomatic high fever and skin eruptions that usually left disfiguring, pitted scars. As recently as the 1960s, smallpox still claimed a fatality rate of 30 per cent in Asia, although large-scale vaccination has now virtually eliminated the disease throughout the world.

ABOVE: *A coin from the British Museum, made to commemorate Queen Elizabeth I's miraculous recovery from the scourge of smallpox. Many of her subjects perished or were left hideously disfigured from the disease.*

# The Gunpowder Plot

ABOVE: *In this engraving by George Cruikshank, Guy Fawkes is shown laying a trail of gunpowder in a cellar under the Houses of Parliament. The lamp he is holding is now in the Ashmolean Museum in Oxford.*

IN THE LOBBY OF THE HOUSE OF COMMONS at the Palace of Westminster hangs an entry from the Commons Journal for 5 November 1605:

'This last Night the Upper House of Parliament was searched by Sir Thomas Knevett; and one Johnson, Servant to Mr Thomas Percy, was there apprehended; who had placed 36 Barrels of Gunpowder in the Vault under the House with a purpose to blow the King and the whole company, when they should there assemble. Afterwards, divers other Gentlemen were discovered to be of the Plot.'

Johnson was the name given to his captors by Guy Fawkes, the most notorious member of the gang of fanatical Catholics who had conceived the Gunpowder Plot, a spectacular plan even by modern terrorist standards. However, Fawkes and his fellow conspirators were not a highly trained assassination squad, but idealistic amateurs enraged by James I's failure to respect their religion.

LEFT: *Every year before the State Opening of Parliament, Yeomen of the Guard perform a ceremonial search of the cellars beneath the Houses of Parliament. To date, no latter-day Guy Fawkes has been discovered.*

The Powder Treason, as it was then called, had little chance of success, soon coming to the attention of Sir Robert Cecil, the king's Chief Minister, who cunningly waited and then pounced at the crucial moment. Fawkes was imprisoned in the Tower of London and the outraged king authorized torture in order to extract a confession to enable the other plotters to be captured. 'The gentler tortures are first to be used unto him and so by degrees to the worst – and so God speed your good work,' commanded the vengeful monarch, who interrogated Fawkes himself.

Fawkes suffered the excruciating agony of being manacled and hung by the wrists for many hours from the wall of a gloomy subterranean torture chamber beneath the White Tower, before being returned to his cramped cell in the Bloody Tower. The tormented Fawkes endured the pain of the manacles, but his resistance was broken after he was brutally stretched on the rack. Finally, on 31 January 1606, Fawkes was dragged through the streets to Old Palace Yard at Westminster, and he was hanged, drawn and quartered outside the very place he had tried to destroy.

The gunpowder proved to be decayed, and would never have exploded.

BELOW: *Robert Catesby, leader of the Gunpowder Plot, together with his fellow conspirators including Guy Fawkes (properly Guido Fawkes), who had previously fought with the Spanish in Continental Europe.*

BELOW: *The notorious 'Little Ease' cell at the Tower of London, where Guy Fawkes was confined for 50 days in exceedingly cramped conditions prior to his execution for treason. He was only 36 years old.*

ABOVE: *James I/VI, the protestant king whose refusal to respect Catholicism provoked the Gunpowder Plot. There is some evidence that the plot was actually a hoax engineered by the state to discredit Rome.*

### SHOOT-OUT WITH THE SHERIFF
Hearing of Guy Fawkes' capture, most of the other conspirators – including their leader, Robert Catesby – fled to the country and barricaded themselves within Holbeach House near Dudley in Staffordshire. Here, on 8 November, they were besieged by Sir Richard Walsh, the High Sheriff of Worcestershire, and a group of vigilantes. After a short, sharp fight, all the conspirators were either killed or captured.

ABOVE: *Coughton Court, Warwickshire, home of Robert Catesby's mother. Coughton was rented by Sir Everard Digby, one of the plotters, as the headquarters for the uprising planned to take place after Parliament had been destroyed.*

# The Jacobite Rebellion

IN THE SUMMER OF 1745, Charles Edward Stuart, better known as Bonnie Prince Charlie, landed on the west coast of Scotland with seven companions. Charles was the grandson of James II, the last Stuart king, and had been exiled in Paris. His aim was to raise an army and restore the Stuart monarchy.

In England, the Stuarts were a distant memory; much of Scotland was prosperous and contented, and only in the Highlands, where poverty bred hatred of English rule, could the prince expect to find support. Even here, many of the clans were indifferent or downright hostile. 'When he came to Skye, my ancestor sent him packing. We had provided 400 clansmen for the Battle of Worcester, yet received no thanks,' declares John Macleod, present Chief of Clan Macleod, talking of 1651 as though it were yesterday.

*Loch Scavaig and the Cuillins convey the appropriately romantic image associated with Skye and Bonnie Prince Charlie – 'Carry the lad that's born to be king,/Over the sea to Skye.'*

ABOVE: *The moon rises over the Glenfinnan Monument in the Western Highlands, where Bonnie Prince Charlie raised the Jacobite standard in his bid to restore the Stuarts to the throne.*

RIGHT: *Charles Edward Stuart, the Young Pretender, painted between 1739 and 1745, the year of the Jacobite uprising. His father, the Old Pretender, son of the deposed James II, had previously plotted an abortive uprising in 1715.*

When the Jacobite standard was raised at Glenfinnan, the prince's forces numbered little more than 1,000 poorly equipped troops. 'Some had swords over their shoulders instead of guns, some pitchforks, some bits of scythes upon poles, some old Lochaber axes,' noted an onlooker as the ragged army marched south.

Fortune favours the brave. The English were caught by surprise and defeated at Preston Pans. Edinburgh was captured. Gathering support, the Jacobites invaded England. Many English troops were fighting on the Continent, and when Charles reached Derby there was panic in London. However, the Highland chiefs demanded to return to Scotland. A long retreat ended on Culloden Moor, near Inverness. Here the Duke of Cumberland's well-equipped army, which included many Scottish soldiers, outnumbered the exhausted Highlanders two to one. The last battle on British soil was over in 40 minutes; the terrible slaughter earned the duke the name 'Butcher Cumberland'.

*ABOVE: The Battle of Culloden was fought just south of Inverness. The Highlanders, worn out after an all-night march, faced into a freezing blizzard as they confronted the English army's vastly superior forces. The result was inevitable.*

The prince fled. After five months as a fugitive, he escaped to Skye, aided by Flora Macdonald, before returning to France. The Highlanders suffered great hardship for many years to come.

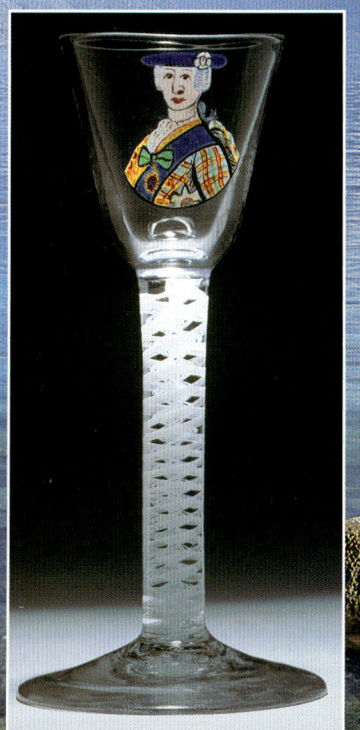

### LEGACY OF A REBELLION

The time-honoured clan system was abolished and it was forbidden to wear the traditional kilt. Large areas of land were given to English landlords or those Scots who had remained loyal to King George. This harsh act, known as 'the Clearances', forced many poverty-stricken Highlanders to emigrate to America. Meanwhile Bonnie Prince Charlie lived out a disillusioned existence in an alcoholic exile.

*LEFT: This glass is part of a set of six commissioned around 1775 by Thomas Erskine, later Earl of Kellie, one of a group of aristocratic Jacobites who met annually to celebrate Bonnie Prince Charlie's birthday.*

# The Traitors from Trinity

IN THE EARLY 1930s, four highly gifted students met at Trinity College, Cambridge, and fell in love with Communism. Recruited to spy for Soviet Russia, they penetrated the heart of the Establishment and became the most reviled traitors in modern Britain. Their names were Guy Burgess, Donald Maclean, Kim Philby and Anthony Blunt.

Their motives appear to have been ideological. In the 1930s, Hitler was in the ascendancy, and, since the British government appeared indifferent, the four felt it was up to them to act decisively. 'To fight fascism you have to be a communist,' was their misguided justification for plotting against their nation. During the Second World War, Russia was allied with Britain against Nazi Germany, and by the time the Cold War had exposed the Soviets' utterly ruthless regime – more people were exterminated by Stalin than perished in the holocaust – it was too late for the Cambridge quartet to repent.

ABOVE: *The 15th-century clock tower at Trinity College, Cambridge, where four notorious spies met in the years between two world wars. Arrogant and totally contemptuous of the nation's political leadership, they collectively became traitors.*

ABOVE: *Donald Maclean as a young man. After he had defected, he became disenchanted with life in the Soviet Union and drank increasingly heavily. His long-suffering wife, Melinda, finally left him to live with Philby.*

LEFT: *Guy Burgess relaxes in the sun beside the Black Sea in southern Russia – the spy who came in from the cold! Burgess later drank himself to death in Moscow.*